Kevin Killian
Argento Series

with a foreword by
Derek McCormack

Pilot Press
London

'Here is Kevin Killian, pounding with bloodied fists on Poetry's door. My heart swells with pride as I claim his masterpiece for our beleaguered city. *Argento Series* is Kevin's *Lament for the Makers*, a monument reaching half-way to the stars for our fallen stars *and every big dream of the world lost to AIDS*.'

Robert Glück, author of *Margery Kempe*

'Lush, tossed off and incisive, there's no other American poet who lived more vividly on the page of his time and its culture—center, edges all of it. Kevin's *Argento Series* is a treat and a complete fact. Grab this volume, fast.'

Eileen Myles, author of *Chelsea Girls*

'High weirdness, thorny beauty, cruel loss – it's all here, in Kevin's voice, and always will be. We will never stop needing this book.'

Anne Boyer, author of *The Undying*

'What Jackson Pollock said of himself, I will say of Kevin Killian: he is nature. *Argento Series* takes its title and frame from the Italian horror film maker Dario Argento but the effect is 100% Killian. Which is nature itself. *Argento Series* was written out of the carnage of the AIDS crisis. The poems are haunting, somnambulant, aggressive, plaintive, uncompromising, sullen, hilarious, brilliant, and outraged, creating a dynamic theatre of true horror. *Argento Series* now takes its place alongside the other queer masterworks of San Francisco poetry, including: Robert Duncan's *The Opening of the Field*, John Wieners's *The Hotel Wentley Poems*, and Jack Spicer's *Language*. It's important we have this title available again for new readers.'

Peter Gizzi, author of *Sky Burial*

'At once tender and terrifying, *Argento Series* is a dispatch from the end of the world. Moving through Italian horror, memories of lost friends, and the long shadow of the AIDS crisis, Killian finds a language for the impossible. This collection is as urgent and vital as ever, seeing the light of day after being unobtainable for far too long.'

Sam Moore, author of *All My Teachers Died of AIDS*

'Through the fake horror of Dario Argento's *giallo* movies, legendary writer and editor Kevin Killian captures the true horror of living through the AIDS crisis. 'The poetry was in the gore,' Killian writes, and these poems are unsane, trembling, lesioned, possessed; horrorcore whimsy, rotting camp. With all the mordant, adrenal wit of a slasher movie's final girl, his *Argento Series* is a survivor's story, vividly retold.'

Diarmuid Hester, author of *Nothing Ever Just Disappears*

for Kathy Acker
Dodie Bellamy
Scott Heim
Steven Shaviro
Gary Smithson and
Juliana Spahr

through whom in the first place I read the work of Dario Argento

"I saw something important I can't remember"

Foreword by Derek McCormack

STAGE FRIGHT... 12

    The Bird with the Crystal Plumage
    Giallo
    Tracking Shot
    Deep Red
    Profondo Thrilling
    Integral Hard
    Trauma
    Phenomena
    Perche Quelle Strane Gocce di Sangue sul Corpo di Jennifer?
    Fiat Croma
    Probability Zero
    The Black Cat
    "K"
    Tenebrae, with Dodie Bellamy

I CAN'T SLEEP... 38

    Udo Kier
    Cat o' Nine Tails
    Suspiria
    House of Wax
    Il Tram
    Testimone Oculare
    The Flowering Face
    Scott Street
    Inferno
    Unsane

Creepers
Cemetery without Crosses
Four Flies on Gray Velvet
La Setta

TODAY IT'S ME—TOMORROW YOU! . . . 66

> The Inn of the Red Leaf
> Goblin
> The Stendhal Syndrome
> Opera
> The Door into Darkness
> Bad Blood
> Trussardi Action
> Daria
> Who
> Zombie
> The Phantom of the Opera
> Today It's Me . . . Tomorrow You!

AURA'S ENIGMA. . . 92

FOREWORD

Yes, the rectum is a grave—but what about the recto?

Argento Series by Kevin Killian has the most fantastic, fucked-up line: "You know how you're reading a book/it's good, the pages on the right/ grow thinner."

Argento Series is more than a good book, it's great. It's sick: its rectos, its right pages, are symptomatic. If the pages are wasting away while we read, then we have to ask: What's wasting them? It's AIDS.

Argento Series is Kevin's AIDS book. It's full of AIDS. I mean: it actually has AIDS. It's the most fantastic, fucked-up thing: it's as if the book's been infected by infected semen, spit and blood. If it frightens you, then forget it; if it doesn't, then finish it—by the end the recto pages will be as thin as Bible paper and mucus membranes.

It's also a book of poems about AIDS. It's full of poems about people— fags, for the most part—who got infected by infected semen, spit and blood. Its poems are full of names, some famous, some not: poets, painters, performers, all fucked, all fucking dead. It reminds me of that Leonard Cohen line you all know: "There is a crack in everything/That's how the AIDS gets in."

My foreword concludes on a recto page—will my words fall ill, too?

Kevin published *Argento Series* in 2001. He'd been looking for years for a way to address the disaster of AIDS. He found it in Dario Argento, the Italian filmmaker. He decided to write about AIDS by writing about the *giallo* films Argento made from the 1970s through the 1990s, *giallo* being a genre of horror. He decided to do this because he saw in Argento's *giallo* films the violence and vileness that AIDS inflicted on its victims, as well as the violence and vileness that society inflicted on those victims.

So this is a work of ekphrasis, though since Kevin Killian wrote it, perhaps we could call it ekkphrasis, or perhaps eekphrasis—it's horror, after all. It seems simple: Kevin describes Argento's work in words. It's not that simple: as Kevin seeks to capture it, the work seeks to capture him. It's the work, it's Satanic—Argento's *giallo* films are transfused with sex, savagery and supernatural spells—and blood, buckets of it. Was there any chance of Kevin writing something about it that wasn't Satanic? Why would he want to write something that wasn't Satanic?

This is a Satanic book—it's the STI in Satanic. Think of it with AIDS. Think of the ekphrasis as fucking, as a sort of swapping of semen, spit and blood. Kevin got what he wanted from Argento: an ambience of brutal bloodiness; in kind, he gave Argento AIDS. That is: he gave Argento's oeuvre AIDS. That is: there's no way to watch Argento's films now without seeing AIDS in them. The disease penetrated into them through these poems: it's like when vampires suck blood from victims and then the victims suck blood from vampires. It's not ekphrasis but something like it—for *Dracula*, we could call it neckphrasis; for *Nosferatu*, Max Schreckphrasis.

Who made AIDS, the Devil or Dario Argento? Thanks to Kevin, we see that Argento's films wrote the story of AIDS *avant* AIDS. This is a source of their supernaturalness: some of these films preceded the poems as symptoms precede diagnoses. This is a source of their scariness: some of these films recorded the horror of a disease that had not yet come. This is a source of their *suspiria de profundis*: it doesn't matter if you haven't died yet—you're as good as dead; it doesn't matter if you were stabbed or bled dry in barbed wire—you died of AIDS because AIDS infected death; it doesn't matter how old or young you were when you died—you died young of AIDS because AIDS made death young.

Derek McCormack, 2023

STAGE FRIGHT

The Bird with the Crystal Plumage

Hey, *goombah,* c'mere,
I've built a flotilla of words to this
        vein in your arm!

Hola, guy, who used to
IV a grow horn in my
        vitals, come on, *andale,*

Here's the big bird
I've built out of crystal
        very cool and white and wet, a swan

high above San Francisco
in a clear winter—
        vite, vite!

Hop on my back
I'll take you there to
        volunteer for the Shanti Project

Happy trails
In the skyways American
        valedictory flock, geese

Help me, I think
I'm falling in looooooooooooooo-
        -ve with you

Giallo

Cut to theme music: brass, strings, zither, giallo
the word bursts in red spectacular fire, soon
muted to a dull yellow like mustard

It's the angle, it's the hook they keep telling
me in the front office, in New York, demons eat them
Wal, blow me down with one of those new fangled

Ok, thought of something bound to beat the
bandolero: mod two in white—battle—killer in the
rain, and the white, wet, reveals shadowy skin

looking like sexuality
talk to Mr. Gabriel
get those asses into those seats

then he gives her a blowjob
the camera pulls back, way, back, sky high
it's a football field of dead men in trenches

doesn't look so scary
it's not like Juliette Lewis
no, it's musical, with glockenspiel
telling the people, *go home now, I love you,*
your breath makes me love you,
in AIDS is pleasure

Steve Abbott told me, when we go we
go into a blank space, like an envelope,
on our way to who? Are you Kevin? he asked me.
The bed a big waste basket of white cotton.

Tracking Shot

The job unfinished. The killer's POV. Long hair blowing in the wind (nameless) an excellent target for bazookas. Thunderous goblin music.

At the moment between now and falling asleep the ghosts rush in. I'm 45, time for ghosts, the dead fluttering their scarves

like Isadora. Duncan. Snap. Head popped off, sails across the screen like popcorn fresh in the big glass warm box, boy's nose pressed against it watching

to the thunderous goblin music. Grabs the boy, curiously not kicking, perhaps a bundle of rags, and drags him up the side of the house

across the roof, avoiding the mansards

down the other side of the house. Through the east windows the beautiful woman is writing her name on a misted porcelain surface with her last breath

I blow on it, the text disappears, the name of the killer.
Up over the house. "I'll call him my 'HOUSE BOY,'" the killer laughs, to thunderous goblin music. Maybe it sounds more realistic in Italian. I hate it when they can't afford real babies or boys

and have to use dummies made of rags, you always know
that's not a baby

the cold air fills the hot wet room like an eraser blanket, now I can't read the killer's name. All she can write is H

and looked at it another way it is I

and upside down, kicking, V

I am reading these signs of the infidel hates me

Deep Red

Deep red • the submarine blips on the cold surface
in Antarctica • as Mariner's ship draws near •
frothy surface on the blue wave •
Life is still • so catch as catch can • still evanescent, still

Red, an oar touches the water's rim • muscular arm buff as
Meryl Streep's in *The River Wild* • in Antarctica •
frothy surface on the blue wave • life is still • "I don't have
many T cells left, but I used to have 8" • "now I have 9"

Under the gristle, vein, under the vein, deep red •
the blood of my pal • deeper and deeper this tiny wave, blue
on the surface, • alone on the surface •
if you were one-dimensional what would you see?
a one celled mammal swimming for dear life •
to a shore strewn with protozoa bracken • still life
"now I have six"

the flotsam and • jetsam of living • high
and deep • this is the curve that
will kill you • pal
I'm living in • your disgrace
deep • red hatchet • cells
a doll with hands • scuttles across the face •
of the sea for you
come and get these • memories

PROFONDO THRILLING

Now the things that are coming to an end,
who will believe them?
Preposterous mettle, cheeky pets,
he hid them all in the date palm,
while I searched the landscape
the moving portrait
which bled real tears into gullible goblet

When I was twenty-one he was always
there a step older then my soldier
on the streets of Greenwich Village in
jelly shoes, tiger lilies, questions
for Laura
The voice in the suitcase
a man darker and older than

the rainbow, in puddle of oil, Bleecker Street
gutter. You know how you're reading a book,
it's good, the pages on the right
grow thinner,
you don't want it to end, there's a clue
right there in the patchwork quilt,
baby let's swing

Long, red, ropy kind of stiff statuary
Where is the night lustre?
Past my sorrows,
rafting down on the glory river
where I searched for his trail,
the living ball
that glowed an unearthly silvery prick—

Stomach, colon, brain acting up, and
over in Berkeley a magic school
I met him on a Sunday
and he taught me how to skip
week days, smoking his weed, whack,
seven strange clues
to guide me to a future sickness, a child

Least he had the grace to look ashamed
his whole broken-ass mule train
Foolish burro of the north lands,
why do you shy away at strangers?
What's the worst that could happen?
The haunted attic
over your headdress files you under—

I feel it in the ocean, often, the unthinking wave,
Surf white and brown in caps, like
mushrooms that come alive then plink
Red-yellow honey, sassafras and
. . . then it's winter,
black mouth moves in the talking snowman
"Ah, Kevin, you're so jejune"

Brrrr! Talk about frosty! I met him on
the breadline, giving him enormous
kicks in the ass
I never wanted to go, but noting
the strange likeness, moved toward him
like two bananas from the same
clump in bodega

hot summer patchouli night stand
with silver bangles cooling Spanish Harlem
fourth floor porch
ghost parade, shadows vanish
so there I am, egg on my face and
unbelievable growing rock, slowly
erect at a dance I hide with my coat flap

—profondo thrilling— Now the
things that are coming to an end
there is nothing beyond them
but surrey
Wait, buddy boy! Invisible chimes
hang from the theater ceiling, safety curtain
let it come down, thud, swish,

plop. Execution completed,
on the bare stage a man lies dead, his
body a motley of harlequin lights
and black diamonds.
Hide your heart, the yellow phantom
whispers at the corner of the curtain
Places please

INTEGRAL HARD

Down in the south land, where every dick
with a woody thinks he's a stickman

along the white pines, Manolo,
we hauled the white pine of Manolo.

Along the white way a man is dead
in the sorry summer of San Tanquera

Manolo, where did he fall
the operation you paid for, with Blue Cross,

your white pine to coffin-size whittled,
Manolo, as though you were a scion of ABBA?

Should the summer heat melt your ice to sweat
sweet as the yellow pine of Manolo Station,

the suppurated halfway of hair pie
where white, once mentioned, Manolo,

peels from the very bottom of the pile-up traffic
in San Tanquera's loco. I stop and cup my ear:

"White pine! Yellow pine!" howl the dogs
of San Tanquera assaulting Manolo

from either side of the one street in hot town
with one pie, and only two dogs with any hair

as Lee, Senior, falls to the floor
I remember ringing your bell and startled

by the way I'd seen Charles before, on TV,
from Mexican westerns, *Star Trek* re-runs

and frail as you were, Matias and I staring
into one mirrored wall, our society gaze

bouncing to and fro ever diminishing
and poetry, a solid stone on the pine deal table

becoming as the night wore on with much wine
ever so much more solid, the thing itself

outside the hacienda a hairless dog long as
dick itself, Manolo, howled to Mars a la

Charles Bukowski and Leland Hickman and
Orson Welles and every big dream of the world lost

to AIDS and its depredations
the Magnificent seven of your wranglers

lonely father on Calle, quiet pierced by gunshot

for inscrutable bush of mesquite, ablaze,

to depredation encircling AIDS like corrida,
"slovenly wilderness,"
until only red molten ring of the poem itself

lies on your doorstep where once I cooled my heels
thinking
"I'm on the doorstep of *fucking Leland Hickman.*"

TRAUMA

I didn't want to have the little boy
but I kept him, tuggled, inside my bush.

You don't eat enough, so you're
spilling your chowder like barley.

Pull over here, I got to hurl my trauma
over the rushing water style bridge bridge,

and watch the series of tiny tugboats
take my baby away the lonesome river.

Trauma of losing a pal to AIDS, or SIDA
as he used to tell me while dreaming.

He was in Barcelona watching the Olympics
like Frank O'Hara in love with Bill Berkson.

Phenomena

Don't make me over, I don't want to lose this strange power of mine
I talk to insects
Arranging trains of locusts and spiders

I take AZT, what's with my complexion, or am I shorter
am I losing
my power of command over the insects

What's worse, this rotten medication that kills you with cramps
or the feeling that
soon the insects will ignore me, I'll be this *dumb fuck*

they can walk all over with six legs and eight legs, I won't
be able to say
a word to them, to alter their course in any conceivable way

I was a pretty girl once in the Basque countryside under
Guernica Ko arabola
the tree of the insects, till the dwarf knifed away my powers

psychic surgery, now I'm caught between two stools
power to live
power to talk to the insects and they will obey me on trains

Perche Quelle Strane Gocce di Sangue sul Corpo di Jennifer?

December 15, Dodie, scornful, "Is he your
        new boyfriend?" I'm humming and hawing, well
what do you mean, I'm not doing him
        "but would you like to?"

January 3rd or 4th, I'm so sure, 1998 and a
        black night in San Francisco
Why did Peter tell Steve and Jennifer I lived
        miles from the Museum, is he trying to
Destroy me? What are those strange drops
        of blood on the body of Jennifer?
What is that bird big as a duck that's not a
        duck on the grass with a black
Bib and dark tan Stripes, is it a kind of dove
        or pigeon? What would I gain
By knowing? Someone seems to have poured
        mineral oil on my new leather date
Book, my "Time Master" trade mark, am
        I coming or going? It's slippery
On the wet surface of our forty steps going
        up, iron piled into flat planes of
Perpendicular, horizontal, all pebbled.

February 25th, Lisa says, "I hear you are
        having row boat weather, I picture
the cats in bright flotational jackets," was
        "Lisa Says" one of the Velvet Under-
ground songs only a fan like I would treasure
        way back when, those endless
canoodlings on a single theme, a woman
        speaking? "Candy" or "Lisa" or
now I can't remember the third. The
        late sixties or 1971. Anyhow the
rain's not *that* bad. Effective but not dismal.
        Beneath my window it's silver
and watchful, like a woman speaking
        in one of Laura Nyro's songs, and

that I can date more precisely. Dodie
would really like to get Marjorie
Perloff to talk about something. Wonder
if the trial has begun, and where?

March 4, Ron Johnson dies at home
(KS).
Waiting
for the other shoe to drop, okay,
clunk. Satisfied? I told him I'd met Peter
(O'Leary), I said, "I love him." His
big eyes shaking under the scars of all
those operations. *"But I really
love him!* Alas, not much I can do
about it." Mystery of the brass bound
trunk with Ron's papers. And today in
ARK I turn to the part about the
grave, O
save me for
the grave who
all the night make I my bed to swim

O
lion, compass
turn
to an end but arrows sing

They speak tongue tried in a furnace of earth,
on every side
I sleep the *sleep of
all*, not
one.

Rebecca and I are true *Wieners* now: eating Sachertorte &
schlag, hot sausages, going to concerts, taking long walks in the
Vienna Woods . . .
[P. O'L]

VENUS. I who am the Queen of Love stand by, powerless,
while he, my son, and she, the girl some called "Venus II,"
lie locked and chained in the powerful transport of love.

PSYCHE. I can't breathe. . . . but what is breath? I never cared to breathe.

CUPID. I can't think. . . . but what is thought? Never had any truck with thought.

    [PSYCHE and CUPID perform enraptured Bolero-type sex dance while Venus continues to sing, and invisible servants enter and mass around her.]

        "Nowadays in San Francisco it's just
fuck, fuck, fuck. I hate men! They're so
        over," Nate tells me. Stood up by FedEx
guy, who wants to bring over whole "hordes
        of men" to have sex while NL watches
I just spent $80 on your ass & you're gonna
        tell me you

rose petals in water glass
Principe

        Dodie meets Mac for a Barber concert
at Herbst Theater. Strange quiet night
        cool fog, on the street, a whisper, hey
homeboy, we stare, the boy smiles wide, his
        mouth is filled with brown vials
capping every other tooth, hey, homeboy
        I'm walking her halfway there
down the concrete corridor to Van
        Ness and Market. Frenchmen
love Cole Swensen: she's so thin and she's
        got that haircut . . .

"Si t'etais beaucoup plus mince, Cole,
        tu serais comme tes cheveux, ou plus mince,
tes cheveux fins d'or."

        Imaginary Frenchman with
bright red coat and small cap. And what is
        with Madonna's new Ray of Light
pre-Raphaelite processed hair, all that
        scalp showing in between? It
feels like a New England hurricane's
        blowing in, the sultry, expanding
air almost bursting with mist, but hot,
        sweaty, the dishes won't dry.

VENUS *(bitterly)*. Look, invisible servants, on this, my mask of
    beauty,
here worn cold as stone in this eyeless palace of night.
It shines! Great beauty shines, yet like the silver moon
eclipsed by the sun's pale orange, it disappears
under the greater force of a children's game.

SERVANTS. Round and round like a child's game tumbles the earth,
fair ball of blue and white, and with it tumbles the sex of this world

Harsh like a ball of red fire, burning each as it goes

Desperate enough to kill a queen, it is the ruling passion of our planet,

And young enough for a boy and girl, and tots of all ages

We, the servants of mighty Cupid, are the toys in his box

He scatters us on the floor in poses ungainly and rude

and when he is done, his mother comes to the bedroom's threshold and
    stares

coldly, as if she were not the Queen of love and beauty.

VENUS. Come, jealous sisters of Psyche, investigate like two Nancy Drews,
sow the seeds of discord in your sister's heart,.
Make her suspicious, make her a crone,
she is too young and lovely like a clover flower.
Wither her fresh vale and dry it like thrash.
What are these strange drops of blood
on the body of
Jennifer?

after James Schuyler & Ronald Johnson
RIP Ronald Johnson

Fiat Croma

He was here one minute, and now
I lie about him, day and night, now
His clothes are pinching
Lobster claws of the dead, while
all the kids are hip

There are no bruises, only KS lesions,
invisible scars in each cell, so the
giant white shot of kelatin
breaks down the resistance
cause it wouldn't be right

to leave your best girl home
and one minute, he was here, cracking
jokes and tails, and the next
I'm clutching the elementary clothes
of the grave, the shroud of

Pinche no? I get bugged driving
up and down the same old strip,
and they leave us alone, striking
the tension, pill after pill so that
you hate Evian water, my

lips are chapped, my feet are bright—
some kind of athlete's foot they
give to these guys, who never did anything
athletic in their *lives,* it's like
this *bonus Fiat Croma*

Probability Zero

Talking to my friend Emily, whose drinking

the corpses change but the party goes on forever,

flat tax soars while it's true, I haven't yet seen vaccine

In the interim he's puffing up, like a large green bullfrog

on the lily pad of the hospice, wet eyes yellow and glaucous

burning holes through the visitor

Probability zero, but don't let a sordid fatalism

give you that Monica Lewinsky fifth amendment

until there's a cure, but from what deep pockets

does the money appear   When you're sick, the last

thing in the world is

Fit, the false falls into place, but sick

I don't know, but an erratic passion blows into our world

and I wilt a little, like Christmas pudding

I don't know, where was I when everyone else I know

was getting bushwhacked, the bullshit of Clinton

In America, the probability's zero, —like weather,

like the inane weathermen on Tv who tell you a

hot front and a cold front are moving into

a clearing, where I could be my "self,"

rituation normal

all fucked up, rnafu, or a "system is moving in"

and we're supposed to feign interest or terror—

while "watching" the "weather"

as years ago Tim died, the man who, whom

I once thought the FALCON MALTESE of sophisticated

and he did not love me but I was not worthy

His black glasses shiny like something alive,

the way that men do,

the way cattle do. He had a vision

I longed to share. His body was not so

pre

possessing. Probability zero that I would live

and he, Tim, his student ID the cover on his book,

would study death before I got to do him

I like felt this stab in my head

a red explosion of blood vehicles, brain flack,

infinitely painful as little by little he

always integral to my sense of myself

as a possible poet began to disintegrate

away across the wide border red ribbon swath of the US

away from me and, in time,

away from kissing him 1979

ten minutes later he spotted a rainbow

even then hoary cliche of gay experiential camaraderie

but, yikes, real—thin ribbon over Brooklyn

Look away, look away

this stormy river

after Tim Dlugos and in his memory

The Black Cat

Lucky cat, pets are people too,
        when you stroke me I wonder, God, what about that FIV?
—the HIV cats come down with . . .

                Come cuddle with me while it rains, a black, tropical
                      rain here,
                in the silver city

Tell me . . . with your paws tap out whose bones are piled
        on the inside of that dark drywall
wet now and stained with the blood of him

        him whom I loved, whom I don't know if,
                if those old bones
        might once have lived inside his castle of

                The castle of his skin, proud and stupid
                      moving in manifold directions, away
                away from me, black cat, tell me . . .

        tho' FIV slows your taps to pats, free me up
                out of this castle of him where he flew for cover,
        then slowly, dot dot dot

"K"

He kissed me, he is not worthy, to join the
KSW, and so is a slow
kick in the head, I will soak him
in kiwi fruit lube for his nasty
Klinefelter's syndrome[1]

"Knowing me, knowing you," un-hunh
keep his kerry off of my
Kidderminster, will you, his
knuckleball endures, his
kohlrabi wilted in my
little kitchenette, when he

kissed me, and it felt like a
keynote address, he
killed me, his swollen kestrel
in my keg—of ketchup brand beer

I'm not worthy of his
constant kelp, the ketone shining in his
kangaroo pouch, give me strength
kind sir, or the kilt of his
kinsmen

I'm living in his regard
His kumquat is my Picard, he
kissed me and it felt like
kimchi in a kiln

---

[1] the severe shrinkage of testicles due to abuse of ketosteroids

Tenebrae

The poetry was in the gore, but in the American version the gore was cut out. Flat. How could these wet souls not love seeing through the specular glass? The blood, spattered over the kitchen cabinets.

Daria Nicolodi, a woman with a flip and a face as long as California, her raincoat flapping in the dark wind. Blue and magenta shadows bleed like what's not there. What happened?

Red stiletto heel in the raw mouth of the youth. The beach becomes a book, becomes a murder. I want to write a poem as long as California. "I didn't do it! I didn't do it!" Her body hurls through the plate glass, shards of undoing, dark pulsion glinting, the body unwound. A thousand holes like seeds, here in the seedy part of Rome. She takes a dagger in a darkroom, O heart of mine.

Revision. Victims emerge from the bath, unsane. I can't see their faces, but their sharp chemical beauty evaporates in the red air.

(with Dodie Bellamy)

I CAN'T SLEEP

Udo Kier

The boy, dead on the forest floor:
rough tongue of deer licking his face, salty as sugar.
Spindly legs of deer, spindly as origami:
his body, wasted and angry in death.
Who is that boy, Rick Jacobsen, why do I see his face
lying still, pale, in the forest glade?
Overhead a bland ceiling of green leaves, sun poking through
Onto the glade of black, gritty dirt, pine smell.

"Rick Jacobsen, this is Udo Kier."
Rick Jacobsen, his red hair stained with sap and mousse.
Deer stand on spindly legs counting his freckles,
His corpse found awkward in baggy ACT UP style shorts, big shoes,
                                        unlaced:
rich clothes fit over angry thin body,
human body now food for a forest of foragers.
Big owl in treetop high, hoots out his name, "Red boy,"
signalling four-legged predators. Red in tooth and
claw-footed they stagger like walking tables;
in silence they approach, not to honor the dead
but to shorten the world, thumping the floor
at midnight, so that by daybreak,
Jesus, you see all these deer licking his face.

Tongues pry open his pale eyelids slightly:
Rick's blue eyes blank but filled with green sun, forest light
where Ernest Hemingway prowled these big woods
where I introduced Rick to Udo Kier
giggle
the mad giggle of Udo Kier trying to speak English at a party
at Brett Reichman's opening at Rena Bransten gallery
and he signed my autograph book
he wrote that he loved me

Up in country outside of Wisconsin
with a big dog, the body heaves
tumbled aside by bear and game, outside of law.

His dirty face, now clean and wet, now streaked with mud;
his eyes and mouth jewels on the floor of the forest,
till, barrel first, a gun pokes between the trees

Udo's not so bad, not a bad shot
like masters, the deer go down, one by one
like falling trees down go the deer
If I did love thee in my master's stead
with such a gamy grin, my lips pulled back in rictus,
I would not understand it,
in my denial thou would see no sense

Cat o' Nine Tails

Karl Malden is blind, a girl of ten
leads him in the dark

Karl Malden blind, he creates crossword puzzles
outside the juridical system

Because the NEA is dead his
dick is ten feet long because
the gene runs rampant in his member
the dick of life, clumsy manifesto
to follow my tails of causing this, that
the other
On the rooftop I turn to you
and think,
I could push him off the roof

then a second thought scatters me like
like parsley

green dry freckles scattered in the
Washington wind, parsley flakes

Scott O'Hara died, the tattoo "HIV +"
bright on his shoulder
so you would know, so he would
inspire Sex Panic
not much of a writer, a video star
so Mark said, at Orphan Andy's, do you
actually know him, he's famous

now locked in the tomb
with Karl Malden, sharing cold cocoa, muttering

The cream it freeze, a muddy brown and gray on
top of the cocoa
Every tail pales compared to the elders
—push him under the gray wheels of that moving train

I'm looking askance and the evil cat
follows my gaze with yellow

Is there evil in the ways and making of man
I believe that out of a biological
warfare experiment gone wrong

US

Suspiria

I know when he began to dance with me
cranberries started to burn in pocket—
I smelled red smoke of sugar under my
feet, sugarfoot, a boy worth burning for—

and into his pants I'd push my white hands,
deeper into the sweeter red currant
in a darkened cell until he was done;
then into a lit cell, where I was king

if music played we sat down fast, out, down
into the red fruit mashed in my lap like
Turkey. Musical chairs with the pilgrims
who came here on the rock to fuck him good

Oh Bill, if you were living at this hour
I'd put little socks on your two bare feet
and spoon this dressing into your wet throat
till you choked and spat all over my bib

I'd give you such a gift of red white meat
you wouldn't be able to sit for a week
unless to eat at the mantelpiece with clock,
bawling pilgrims thrusting your ass with fire

ferret teeth in the breast of a red bird

I would call it to your memory now
that a phantasmal fog of love had enthralled me to you

then, but not only then, in these my words
the tear in the fabric, now, *the drop of blood.*

House of Wax

Her spooky face is bent.
under the twisted apple blossom.
She takes your hand and gives it a wee squeeze,
awake, you scatter her ashes under
the twisted apple blossom.

"We're nothing but lab rats,"
she gasped,
drugged tubes piercing up her throat, like thorns,
leaky thorns, twisted brambles
but pure and white and red.

Men pull her toward the morgue.
Under the stinging white lights of the ray
techie type gowns hold out hands of salt
refresh us, they beg, in the house of
wax, the melting wax her body makes.

Give me back her floating eyes
I'll put them in my shadow box
and build a new face around them
smiling and screaming
mouth open, apple blossom falling from it
come on and let it snow

Il Tram
for Dennis Cooper

There are six of us on this tram
before we get to Minna Street
one of us will be murdered!

First I was Invisible Girl
then Wonder Woman
and now I am Thief Catcher

And who are you, she firmly spoke
When men fly over your
head I'm hatcheting ratcheting

Copy your sums
onto the ancient oaken bar
separating public from private tram riders

and pay your piper
Necklace of pearls
Lost down the piano wires of big Italian tram

Playing music as it approaches
our little alley
and the killer strikes glissando

Invisible Girl can you see him
Thief Catcher snatch his rat ass up
let's bar B Q him on Minna Street

Cough up those pearls
his wounds plugged with pearls
which when removed are washed

Asia Argento thinks she sees
someone she saw in the tram
humble down cobbled alley

no cloak but the night
his pearl like face a ghost face glow
over his shoulder as I snatch

up his rat ass
I copy my sums on said rat ass
breaking down wall between public

I don't know how you feel
about Ewan McGregor said Dennis
but after watching *The Pillow Book*
you get bored with his perineum

Testimone Oculare

"I saw something important
that I can't remember"

Trailing the earwig
in one ear and out the other, too late
it's laid eggs, they crack apart
inside the slowly pumping brain

Conventions of horror demand a nut,
eyewitness, whose eyes can't be trusted,
but the life I've lived—gross,
the deracinated heart, pumping dully on a lead table
keeps faithful record of the life I've lived

The tortured, the abused, the egare,
the lonely and eclipsed, the lost
Edina says to June, "I'm taking recovered
false memory therapy, I'll get something on you yet!
You in a hood in a wood—

it's all coming back to me now," on
Absolutely Fabulous. I saw something
important that I can't remember, for
the eyes wear no face, no memory strand

while inside the brain the earwig twins
grow in the dark, luminescent, toasty.
One vigorous shake of the head
should kill them, but "I want you to be:
volo ut is," as Augustine said

for Avital Ronell

The Flowering Face

He read all his poems twice, thinking,
        "they did not hear them the first time."

They hired a team of gay men who do this
        gardening gig to do it for them.

If his body rots in the mouth of maggots
        let's go to Zuni

Down his throat
        poured a river of beer and rum

In the coercive moonlight of Diamond Heights
        his red hair, gold

He'd like the symbolism
        and of course the spring flowers

He was subtle, always said, "Hello my friend,"
        as though he knew us better than indeed he did

If the words I wrote, and throw up into the sky, in his direction
        mean what I think they do

Then deep into the black earth a post I dig, that says
        retention must be paid

I found out who he really was
        through the name on the bracelet, pink and white beads

A couple of guys from Ireland
        passing through town and one says, "Die faggots"

If there was no poetry there would be no
        toy, face, torment, healing, gladiola, prix fixe, heaven

Scott Street

And when I turn and you are not here
Only a habit, like cyclamen, to
turn to the sun

Goodbye dear, you are not for me,
You have turned at last into the sun
like moss of glassy green, a wave

But it was just one of those things
"The butterfly, my soul grown weak"
over the lamp, a green cloth

Moss dripping in shade
                              twilight here
Moss past the moon, to tear away the

Wax from your chest, each tiny
hair screaming. If when I turn
To you as so often in the pasture

And you are not here, I've got a
new kick   he works as a waiter
in the restaurant on Scott Street.

This shiny tip I might have left for
you I hand to him to insure proper
service and to get him high.

He's coming up the stairs, I suppose,
to take away the broken-hearted
memories of your coated black tongue

Needle sharing programs
dictated by Uncle Sam here on
the corner of Scott and Prince
in San Francisco back porch

The poem never says what lives in the barrel,
clear as his green eyes, no mirror
for the drug we ingest

Always a shot to the blood,
condom, dripping over the edge of cracked toilet seat,
mossy green and hacked up from your chest

In your final memory, I suppose
Why not?
         We live under its law and
You died and he's pounding up the stairs
like his hair's on fire and his ass is catching
Oh Johnny, women in the night
call out yr. name

         after John Wieners

Inferno

Inferno maybe too descriptive
I lived with him for seven years
black under water, a shark on fire

Are you the patient XYZ?
who blew smoke up my ass
and fell into watery aphrodite loving me!

Rip that tube from the wall and feel me up
loving you and forcing you to wriggle a bit
a sausage on griddle, hot

Mother of tears, mother of shadows
give him a little more zip
I don't want him self-conscious
when he walks among dot dot dot

Big, bright colors like a Cibachrome painting
by Nan Goldin should she turn to oils.

I ate the seventies dancing in disco
and made the eighties this fresco experience
Now I'm impoverished, begging

for my birth mark, going on thorazine
should I turn to oils, shark under fire
or should I just say, *tattoo man, make*

me a birth mark, say it was me from the
beginning, and in thy honor I shall
do thee justice? I lived with him when he

died and I'll live when he abrades me
for he is the Saxon justice of a women's
barony, he gives me strength, to carry on

he lights up my life, disco inferno
night falls on a prodigal landscape, loving
him was never light mechanical

Mother of mercy, mother of pain
tell him for me he lives on my derma
when I pull it off gently after the chemo

He won't love me without my foreskin
tiny little snip of waxwork
only a storm toss'd frigate by Turner

Tell him there's some easy pickings
long and low the banks of the Mersey
white Jersey daisies and calla slips

creeping up the inner side of his leg
locks and curl then up to inside his anus
where I admitted the thorazine early

Mother of HIV, mother of envy, grant me
the shallow wish to be loved like a man
in the highest way, la vita nuova, in your

shallow dish I shall take to Goshen
learning the ropes inefficient way, if the
boat don't break don't fix it, miles of

ash and fire all you can see, in your throat,
your naked silver throat, a shallow boom
box, glug, it's coming through and we're

history.

UNSANE

> CHARLES: Your behaviour has shocked me immeasurably, Elvira—I had no idea you were so unscrupulous.
> ELVIRA *(bursting into tears):* Oh, Charles. . . .
> CHARLES: Stop crying.
> ELVIRA: They're only ghost tears—they don't mean anything really—but they're very painful.
>
> —Noel Coward, *Blithe Spirit*

Anyway it was only because I loved you—that's right
So rub it in what high hopes I started out with. Okay
A nightingale
does sing
outside this window

                                    Trying to live my regular life
Touched in the head, a wand exploding on my hairline
Look! I'm 44, I've come through
Okay, so there's now a knock at the door for you
                  my love
With trepidation you answer it

His face is carved from anthracite
His body cloaked in protease inhibitor
        So, net result is, can't see the fog for the trees
        Oh dear, but that is what happens
in the Canadian century
                              sip of water from wet canteen

that I rub over your face, pick up sweat, tears,
and the incorruptible eschatology
of the book you devoured,
                          kins,
a girl worth a million of two thousand boys

        I'm unsane, my books are parked on 101,
        a bird at the window pecking
        hard cold beak-like nose, I'm under your weather
        in romantic Cancun . . . blue field,
        rose stripe

Agnes Martin, her paintings must go for
400, 500 thousand, living in
              immaculate motor court and studying the
patterns of PBS in the dark quiet Taos night
nearby the   mausoleum of Lawrence. You

      can see I've been trying to get through to
      the dead ones—a pierced veil, who broke ranks, *the act of*
          a generous heart. The city fritters in
      fear, of the unsane, approach him with gloves,
      you needn't come down like a ton of bricks

Okay, a masked creature does
approach the window on Jones Street in
San Francisco, the town without graveyards—
      Stymied by your willfullness, I trace
the rim of a beer mug on your beer face.

          They don't mean anything really:
              the tears, the sweat, the semen, that
          flow incorruptibly from the faces of Mary,
          but they're very painful.
              Slouching at this bar helps me work, I swear.
          Stymied by your mouth I bite off your hair.

                        after Robin Blaser

CREEPERS

Night, and they walk unsane, sprawling chins of steel,
the fearless, the torn, the lamentable . . .
freaks of the underworld.
                                    Warm misty moon
high above landing on Minna Street
once a bordello, now
black rubber curtains part . . . to unveil
a silly beer bottle, like a lava lamp
twinkling with smoke and pink fluid . . .
                      always the unsettling memory of
moonlight, sharp and sudden.

                                      When
you were very young, studying TV,
space people go into Mars as boldly
as the creepers who crawl my street . . .
shoes in their mouths, shoes
            in their mouths so no one can scream at them.
                        I've got a line open
waiting by the phone and nothing but
        the bad news of every day
warm misty moon, unseasonable
heat for February, like a scarlet sno-cone
those freaks of the underworld . . .

TV's warm, as though someone
had helped a stranger.   His body,
turned facing the set, tuned to TV,
nineteen stab wounds closing with clotted blood, and vermouth . . .
in an interlingo of clicking glottal stops . . .
and his hands move to the screen, as though the stranger had turned
into a
friend.   "Hello" in English.
Master puppeteer, rods twitching
strings jumping, and the tiring thing is the thing we must do first
sunlight or no, moonlight or no . . .

I'm no expert, though I wish I was, I was more like a man,
in this tiny apartment
living from week to week,
                                      until the steps
on my forty stairs, like thieves, stop,
hold a finger to their teeth, and clamp
on your old brown shoe, a cat in heat.
                  . . . .If I give you my whistle,
you'll yawn . . . .your mouth so open
you could suck on it dry as heaves, scary, like some kind of—
—*pus freaks of the underworld*—
                        street goon stabbing you nineteen
times for money, in your neck and face

Larry Eigner, Bob Flanagan, you guys
were kind of sick before you died, huh?
          Air creeps through the lungs, the tiny
                sore branchials, thievery internet
with no return, up my forty steps
you just stop there dead—I don't want to
with diseases I saw on TV and in the stores,
        tugging on Dad's sleeve whispering, what is
it with those people, Dad? Warm moonlight misty with lotion
on my hands, I see these guys
on the Jerry Lewis Telethon, and two of them
were you. Wheels of a cart
trundle down the stairs to
the alley   the heap of cracked bones

creep down my street, once a bordello,
you two men, flesh rotting off your bones
like tenderized shrimp in the market
always remembering and seeing
         when the clouds disperse
I whistle across the great warm wind like a bunch of creepers
                to wriggle up the steps under my door
into my bed and night dreams
        the seven orifice body loving me for what I am
since you came to California for my birthday, "Oh!
Man! This is *unsane!*"

Cemetery Without Crosses

Things are fine
with me—good writing,
good fucking—Ideal really

Pyramids
to be arranged
in the shape of a cross

Americans
cut up the four hour
Trauma

He's not
so spectacular, I
mean, I'd do him but

And he
is Ronald Johnson
a far cry

How dare
you write me of
fucking somebody else

Valencia Street
rain on your face
ravaged, ruined blood face

O lion, compass
turn
to an end but arrows sing

made
all the dishes
from one of his cookbooks

and he is
Ronald Johnson
name the date

Four Flies on Gray Velvet

Il Marchi di Naescere:
the old dead family heirloom, watch closely as
      Mimsy Farmer, a blond kitten with an American backhand
one more box with me, Mimsy pleads
          in the dying arms of the old box pedlar

Non! He sings with a kind of visionary rapture
tucking cats into sandwiches for the poor
      people of Rome—*Non!* She plays her trump,
a perfect circlet of guitar hole for the masses,
      he eyes it needily, oh Mimsy, shame!

for you are rich as velvet in the gray matter
while he's needy, though what a tenorous bagpipe of love,
      can't you have spent your largesse in a different light? Take
the old surgeon of Rome, he's poor as four flies,
        cradling the enormous *Marchi di Naescere*

while you hack away and blame the stud husband
whose only crime is snooping through demesne.
      Box man shakes his black and white, sorry
but—No! His famous aria, "Non!"
      Not in a million years, Mimsy Farmer!

In a way too bad, since you are only the victim
of a rapacious dad and absent woman thing who cared
      but couldn't cut the mustard, while the very three-
dimensionality of characters doom them
      to moody baby doom a yam, etc.

As one by one, the men I knew and loved, or disliked
leave this planet due to a rapacious virus
      my widow wear gets lots of use
in the middling funeral march hare nightmare
      that's the way of our times, I know, but

how can I keep going, tell me, Mimsy Farmer
the weakness of support, the get well cards unsent
                saquinavir trickles into vein like syrup
the insipid drain of hospital white, wash your hands
     how to keep from screaming as one by one

Ammonia wreaks their joints, a look alike
and death looks more like a person than he used to
            look at me, under the fringe of hair
Or over the raggy edge of an old book of old Foucault theory
      when I had my jacket on, black leather,

gray velvet. When I walked into the crowd, forgetting
my fly was open, and you lingered behind me, pointing
          I have been embarrassed again
by my genitals' behavior, and how they once peeked
        into the face of a world-wide epidemic etc

yet a cat can look at a king, in the films of Dario
Argento, and way to go, Mimsy Farmer for your
            sterling performance in his
strange fever. Nasty patches on my epidermis
      like four flies, on gray velvet, but nothing

La SETTA

The thing described makes a run for it

to the form of the question

Say you were in a cult as a girl

would memories haunt a woman, repressed

The panting footsteps of the thing, described

      a faery ring,

the OK corral, hung with Cady Noland-type

memories of Manson

until blanched hands rip from out of red sand

      the swirling tumbleweeds

and tackle your face in a patchy Italy

needles ring your face like Oberon, a tingle

your face rips off, later

a stud shows his face and a scream

runs ribbons around the world, the thing

described six hundred feet tall,

      and pretty ugly

TODAY IT'S ME—
TOMORROW YOU!

The Inn of the Red Leaf

Robert Duncan: Sonnet 3: From Dante's Sixth Sonnet

Robin, it would be a great thing if you, me, and Jack Spicer
Were taken up in a sorcery with our mortal heads so turnd
That life dimmd in the light of that fairy ship
The Golden Vanity or *The Revolving Lure*.

Whose sails ride before music as if it were our will,
Having no memory of ourselves but the poets we were
In certain verses that had such a semblance or charm
Our lusts and loves confused in one

Lord or Magician of Amor's likeness.
And that we might have ever at our call
Those youth we have celebrated to play Eros
And erased to lament in the passing of things.

And to weave themes forever of Love.
And that each might be glad
To be so far abroad from what he was.

Bring in the prisoner
in black and white telephones, shackles
he will tell what he knows of the red inn of the red leaf
if I am a judge of men

"It's in Canada"
Is that all you can tell us, prisoner of the
black jail in Milan winter?

My tongue torn away by plants
emits a wig and wag, that's all, c'est Leonor fini

The Inn of the Red Leaf
slap his face
make him cough up in blood more details
not just "it's in Canada" do you think us fools!

In the winter of my 45th year
I was on the phone with Dodie
and she said Kathy Acker was very sick

The white washed walls of the police state office
and the sweat of the prisoner
talking without crosses
supported in the chair and thinking these thoughts
with no direction

Who went to Venice, the icy banks of the canal
Who went to Tijuana on the wings of a snow white dove,
now you see her, now you don't
A hora la mira, y a hora no
Waiter! Check into the inn of the red leaf
Accommodate party of large egos with
utmost civility
On New Year's Eve
I'm sitting here thinking, where is she now

Dodie, I would like it if you and I and Kathy Acker
Were all still alive through some Jamaican voodoo herb
And our Filipino healer put us on the fairy boat
like *Pussy King of the Pirates* but with less pressure

A big ship with a white sail that thrills to loud music
And we could not remember who had written what
and who had stolen what passage from another
"our lusts and loves confused in one"

like Harold Robbins filibustering with red face in UK courtroom—
And I'd like it if all the fellows we ever loved
And been dominated by before pirate advent
And the men who died so that we could live and sail

Kind of, you know, were like the slave boys.
And I'd smile to you and you and she at me
To be on this funny sea, this choppy cool violet water.

Goblin

> *I'll have the glass, the shimmering dust*
> *to see the ragged real better*
> *through its shade*
> *and second skin*
>   —Charles Watts, "Dramatic Realism"

I keep waiting for a break, alas—
ten thousand party favors have to be blown up and placed,
just so,
on the table of the zombies of the lake

"Of the," "of the," all this possession
I'm haunted by, built into the structures of English
like that shadow on the dinette table

It is hundreds of years old, and creaks with yellow

Watts up Charlie Chan? I used to say
on the telephone, can I put you on hold,
slamming down before he could say yes or no,
"Now I'm back," but you never know
if the distant person will be there still
breathing

a ferocious guess
the ragged real, and I would say
what's so real
we're just molecules who went to school

> *Each dust point's a blazing prism*
> *the glass a crystal screen*
> *and cast against the glamor*
> *the image, vine and leaf,*
> *of blackberry,*
> *whose body, almost unleaved, thick, still*
> *unwithered, green and armed,*
> *endures the February light a foot away.*

I'm afraid of my face, that gathers in a scrunchie
all of the sights I witnessed in a trance
A round robin of sights
that, once eaten, never graduate
from the Tanz Akadamie of Joan Bennett, Alida Valli
& what is that thing that looks
like a giant slinky
try to escape it, your flesh tears off in liver strips?

Kill a bat, light a cigarette, breathe easy
except for the face pinned to one's skull
Watts up, Charlie Chan, I haven't
got all day
I'm a busy man
More peccable than the boy, still unwithered,
armed, green, the unendured
and a foot away from il lago di zombi . . . darkness

The Stendhal Syndrome

With a rush, and we do away
Look at those Brice Mardens
and the big horses of Susan Rothenberg
and the palette without color of Neil Jordan

Pleasure as a synonym for AIDS
its metonymic attachment to the body
the fringe on top of the surrey of living
easy without you, easy air Jordan

Color my world white, with veiny streaks of red
A terror at giving up my seat at the opera
the family box
I really fucked myself over, that box of steak.

Steel stripes shadow the steel pier—Brighton
Smegma nada, the reverse of what?—My dick
tiptoes through the sands in another's—shoes
a river wide, green desert ribbon—

Opera

The tricky part is keeping your eyes.

Loving isn't enough, not with needles.

Overhead of the crowd beats the black crow,
His chance revenge.

Betty the teenage opera star in her
glittery black and silver Raiders gown
the crow, attentive, tilts his beak to caw
though no sound escapes

My mother slept with him long ago
Now he's back to give me an opera
dedicated to my name
in this theater holy with my death.
Unlucky love, that left to my devices
needed transfusion from lens to lens,
takes off his shirt in deco profusion
giving me head over hand over hand,
unlucky in love, lucky in cars
pull over and pick me up
I'll take you where

I've been watching you since
you were a child
In the corner of the schoolyard playing ball
and reading Wayne Koestenbaum

I've got a van with locks that shoot down into the doors, once you're in
head over hand over hand

Folly to take so limpid a face for a match
the gun droops from your pale hand

give me the gun, dear
I'll bind your green bruises with this ketone acetate,
that freezes into cloth once bound around
an itchy trigger finger

the swelling must go down

van back, cold corrugated metal, scrap of red carpet
put your eye to the keyhole
while the stitches force you to see
that which is unseeable
the collision of the ghosts in the hall
singing an aria, and banging into each other,
their flesh, not flesh, stinging then melting
they pass without speaking, only surprise
the tricky part is keeping your eyes
ghosts pause, behind each other now
do you see them in the dusty hall
see them shimmer, reading Wayne Koestenbaum
the crow, attentive, tilts his beak to caw
a sound escapes

Attention focused on the van
it starts to hump, to rock, its fat black tires
squeezing
and sighing, and swelling

Ink those tires, drive them over white strips of
paper like John Cage and Robert Rauschenberg

Like John "Van" Cage and Robert
"Van" Rauschenberg

The Door into Darkness

A hand within touching distance of the doorknob.
No light, no sound, the lintel black with absence and size.

The wristwatch that talks, "Time for your medications."
Feeling, the cold drip inside your thigh, the scent of fear.

Quiet, the set is cleared and the long spaces grow still, dark.
Bitter scent of attempted, the light, the warm hatching eggs.

Open the door, pick its hinges, flood the house with darkness.
A short burst of steam, the mailbox slot hot as his asshole,

darkness within and the field of the open human page. The
check for his pills, and a glass of water from crystal springs

tipped to his mouth: he is old now, yodelling in a sleep
indecent, cracked, his hand furtive sly yanks at a single sheet—

Pull at the tubes, throw open the black wooden door and let go.
All the world staring at him from inside his own eyes

and I'm like, the hand that takes the door by the knob, firmly,
uprooted, as once I made him come with my hand, till he

couldn't stop gasping for breath. Now he can breathe, now
he can live, now he can come, now he can write "dead" in the
    dark.

Bad Blood

When two people lives in squalor
the dictator among us grins
His snigger subtle as gnome's fingerfuck
Rotting cicada,
imitation rolex worn at the elbow, like his aqualung
worn at the lung
like cough, reflexive cough of Allen Barnett

He's interesting for a year
then you tire of his what.

Did you ever think you'd be seeing him humbled
Not quite there, and even that is sad! Where's the party?
Always thought that maybe, if only, I'd turn on the lights
on the one boy, in the shape of melty copper, his fresh
underwear grinning at his waist in the window—
And now, in the afterlife of Nijinsky, a
mess of pottage I gave up my birthright to anagram:
He is the victor, defeated, spanked.

On the deck he naps, his sorry ass slung in my deck chair
Poetry Princess
from the civil tsi-tsieh of Kim Ki-Young detached as dainty Rottweiler
Well, Sam, it took me ten years to
think of a way to return you from the grave
All bets are off now, we're sailing in an hour
Turn over his Rolex to its backside, read its inscription, from
    Sam to Kevin 1988
and say it's not stolen, stripped from the bony arms drooping off the
    gray metal table—
I can read, can't I? I can be this kind of—
reading person—

KizZool cuz skiZool iz out ÷
It's cool ÷ cuz
school is out ÷
WOW did you ever see even in a museum
such a collection of boddisatvahs ÷ the way
the way they have to sit above the rubber

Or that one was, inside his pants, the Yiddish poet
a vegetarian. Or another—all in his mouth—a snarl
of the Sources. The one I loved most, who once,
once only, let go the pain, the night he got drunk,
and I put him to bed, and he said, Bad blood.÷÷÷÷÷÷÷÷

after Charles Olson

Trussardi Action

Shadow, dart away, let me be, with invisible scissors cut me some slack,
I'm so tired of your trespasses, dark shape that moves in my body—
Lithe and shapely, attractive, wow.
Everywhere I walk, a chill runs across my path like a black cat on fire
Never to be mastered or shifted, here's to whistling in the dark
Clever chill that knows which way I'm coming
Everywhere I walk with you, shadow man.

Even as we speak you're imitating the way I talk
Quarrelling with me by using my gestural pneuma
Under the twisted apple blossom, a shadow falls, not of this earth
And even as I try to have sex with somebody else, you're
Like a virgin
Shut away for the very first time

Dark boy, playing with yourself, contorting my body
Everywhere I go, I'll make you shiver, you'll regret this impertinence
As you follow me, I'll be wearing Trussardi
The clothes of another country, woven from light
Here in the art of another your hands will be forced from my dick
And bound behind your back, your eyes closed
My men will ready, aim, fire
Ho, ho, ho, Henry Higgins, just you wait!

Bullets pierce a shadow,
Hit a wall, that I got to see. Without my assistance you
Couldn't find my ass with both hands, if that's what you call them.
Shadow condensed of the dozens, go now,
Me to live in a world of lanterns, flashing grief from each pore in my
Real body, while yours lies, dead harlequin,
On the black and white carpet of action Trussardi.

Daria

If I had a lira, beyond the Aegean
as you were floating on a dolphin's tail,
salt, silver, your eyes closed to the heavy sun
and I were a transvestite, wearing
the clothes of a woman and the red
high heels of death—
If you didn't like the sex, you had only
to say so many words so glibly, dog-paddling,
I put the headphones on your ears
simultaneous transmission to
the States and to Canada, where
the corn grows higher, and corner, so
if you were my woman and I was
a man, sinking deeper under the dolphin's
funny genitals, into a blue empyrean ringed
with coral cacti and flibbertigibbets
as my grandmother used to say—
what's goose for the gander?
If I were a king and Daria, you could be my
favorite star, the tainted goddess
I wanted to be as a "grown up"—young,
young forever in the house I was born in
only to be yours, lost, rapt, a pretty girl
in heels to bust my eyeballs. Always think-
ing I'd escape from your love—as you;
Sinking, or thinking, could I be you?
Nonetheless you'd leave, me to your card
stained with mud, dark souvenir
of the UFA we both knew as an arid skin
sloughed off in the arid bath of my tears

Who

Who, I didn't love him enough
ninety thousand names for the government
to gamble on, to conjure, out of a hole
so big it could be only

Who said to me *look at my lesions, no,
Kevin, really look, don't look
at the stars
enough of your avoidance behavior*

His body, in state, or tumbled through
a rinse cycle drying in the feathery wind
lint on your net, your intersticed
net, who
I loved so long but not enough

Who gave Steve Abbott the "AIDS Award
for Poetic Idiocy" seven years before he died?
                                        (Ed Dorn)

Who, rather than waiting
seized his little liver in a
silver thimble, the man I mistook for a moulting
hen, I, reigning the roost, the big cock of 1983,
I
impenetrable safe of steel, those
tiny fingers made me look like a monkey

Who on the plush row
of velvet embroidery, Joni Mitchell sobbing
in the pew behind me, "I wish I were a river
I could skate away on," a thirst so deep
confession doesn't cover it

I wanted him to live
to fill his throat with "Mella, mella peto
In medio flumine," but who
was it told me
They are moving his body
into the memorable room of a long love

Who was the mad man who took him back,
while we watched indignant such a man could go
in the front row with Lisa and Dan
watching David Wojnarowicz scream
his spittle on my chin
at the gay bookstore in San Francisco

marvelling at, comparing him,
who did this to me, that I
lived and did so little to be clear
always the quaint uppermost in mind,
my mad strive for personality,
always the quaint peppermint misread
who

made the little tiger the big lamb on Sunday,
broke my will, gave me to the boy
following him down to the grave
holding back, something
ungiven

who launched this rocket into space,
that burst into earth, one death at a time,
its rockets a flare of red and pink pinspots,
livid bouquet in the night sky
over beautiful city
whose garden did I pick this death from?

Zing, zing, a phone insistent
as kismet, the fate that brought me to
a dark reply, hello, is Kevin Killian
home, I've got a message, and
who is this, I whisper into the phone,

who did you say was calling
for him, the straight black mouth
of the plastic phone,
I'll see if he's in
and who did you say, if you did say

and I don't think you did say
who, who took me to this
date in my history, who made my
feet scatter like the burnt leaves of
the oak seedlings, while I walk to
the phone as though nothing
were happening,

under the sky, under the rain, in San
Francisco, home of the birds and the
sun and the big bottle of dilaudin and
morphine I gave to him Sunday
and leaving him, quietly, I closed

the door on my nation

ZOMBIE

Father who keeps one great yellow eye peeled for the
Boy, don't let him grow up to be that peeping Tom
With the German accent. Father of definition, let no

Glaucoma take him behind the screen of white china,
He's my little wriggling thing I eat like a jujube.
Out of your mouth you spewed me like catfish, lukewarm,

Whiskered, "hot diggety dog!" said the other children
Crowding round my genitals as though on Bonfire, but
Then coming back to school to pray, heads bowed

Father who makes this body of sense go stupid
Whenever I see you burning in that berry bush,
Keep your guard down till over your self-defense I leap.

I once did ooze, but now I'm hard, I'll become lard
If a prayerful sort. Dance class at noon, I expect
Every *Mein Herr* to take that duty, dinner at sevenish,

Little gummy green bear assails us at table with news of
Thee, soup on the left, big bowl of snapdragons floating
In the water of Thee. Dear God, as I lay dying of AIDS

I prayed to you and all your ministries nightly and daily,
And you were out in school teaching us the colors of the fag.
Dear God, let me freeze up his serious T-cells into miasma

And bring him alive in the 23rd century, I can't lose
Everything—not in 1 day. Jesus fucking Christ, I'll bring
Corpse after corpse to wash your feet with, to open a closet

With a bullet in space, sleep if you are tired, rest if
You feel trenchant. Father of HIV stop the digital maniplex,
Close your eyes, close your eyes, relax think of nothing tonight.

The Phantom of the Opera

> *Had this been a heterosexual these two boys*
> *decided to take out and rob, this never would*
> *have made the national news. Now my son*
> *is guilty before he's even had a trial.*

His little feet are green.
Take the barrel off the wright
for his green feet. For a load of
chops. Matthew Shepard, 21
Propellor to the stars, the green stars, high over Laramie's
outskirts and weary and back to the base line
the fence on which they found him
a scarecrow

I fell apart when he approached,
a dizzy fog flailing round my skeleton
arms flapping, and used this
to write novels

the beautiful birds this dead boy scared away
the welts forensics took for burns

this weakness—
in intensive care
Nurse figures in transit, and swift about it
Doctor, stat,
> *have you ever seen feet so green*
> *he's been stepping on clover*
> *a piece of state scum*

dunked into a barrel. Boys
said the queen of Minna Street
have you been set upon by thugs
Russell Henderson, 21
Aaron McKinley, 22,
themselves slight,
who robbed you of your underwear

Boy's don't forget me
I've your welfare at heart
said the queen of Minna Street
his pale feet in the rug of their scalp

As they walk away
their asses throb like chlorophyll
shrug

A is for Kevin
B is for missed the bus on O'Farrell Street, standing there, my paper
    and dick
C is for AIDS deaths dropped in half in 1997, now only the 15th killer
    in America
D is for plastic sheets, two men huddle beneath, dancing, performance
        and E is for the night we
saw Louis Malle and Uma Thurman in that restaurant
        and met Kiki Smith

"F," as in Clint Eastwood, hairy stare
    K to the I to the double-L
anagram = Old West action, what do they spell

Matthew Shepard, 105 pounds, five foot two,

"G," —other causes leap out of the pack
    accident, suicide, murder, sign of the cross
        as AIDS drop down to 15
            after 15 years
and murder in Laramie

    "A" is to axe and "H" is to hatchet
"I" is for "iris" and "J" is for "jacket"
He took a long turn to 405,
kept the cure, his neck burnt black
"J" put the stopper in perfume X
took the wheat from the Blistex bottle
"K" for the almost perceptible slur
in your bankbook, I don't remember half
of these guys, that got key-toned

Exist now as letters only—
alphabet mired in gum
"L" is for Matthew, who sat on a fence, scaring crows,
"M" did the wild thing on my dime

The pop art [George Oppen wrote]—a Disneyland tour of Dadism? or the anger, the destructiveness of the homosexual, the totally disconnected, the man without natural valences—to him not only the structure but the purposes of society must seem AT ALL MOMENTS totally absurd.

Black plantain cross rosary plate
on snowy white linen
snarled with your drool
so I keep my books in plastic sheets
I am the little boy who went in
       to the sea to rescue your scarf

from misery heap, picked over by
hungry—
and—
It is true, Christine

I am not an Angel, nor
a genius, nor a ghost

I am Erik

Forget the name of the man's voice

the corpses change but the party goes on forever,

Today It's Me ... Tomorrow You
(Oggi a me ... domani a te!)

Gothic set-up for a dollar climax,
money comes into the room,
the candle disappears.
I'm AIDS'ed out, pockets turned back to front,
inside out, flapping like whitefish
in my white pajamas
We can be like they are . . .
Curse its gilded milkteeth! Dedicate the
grave to Nothing! In the camera's eye
my body moults from feathers
to a tough tensile steel,
reenacting the bird bath of another agent.
Romeo and Juliet
another 40,000 every day come
up the subway steps to New York
Tall gray buildings hot with light
and long rows of the hospital dead
There's a place I know
where we can go and have some coffee
nor do the wind, the sun and the rain
His tots cry around the relict
gorgeous music for a shapely eunuch
his tots now orphans, the ceiling
of paternity lifted off and swept to the
dark sky

Sucked clean, eh.
Out of the night, and just when the plink of sleep
falls out of the dollar
100 percent down coverlet so cozy
white as fluorescence

A low roar, mounting, the mind alone.

"Seasons don't fear the reaper,
nor do the wind, the sun, and the rain,
we can be like they are."

it was an older man showed me
the steps of the dance
I can't forget
tall man whose shoes I
stepped on when
I was trying

to write
before AIDS catastrophe
made writing inequitable
the mind, alone, a corsage
of pink crinkles rather
like the asshole of Tommy
which when

I touched it with my thumb
wet
shivered alive, alert
in Port Jefferson
above a harbor ringed with boats
on the bed a web of his
wet clothes
that's me
thinking

Aura's Enigma
for Juliana Spahr

Aura's Enigma

Dear Juliana,

Dario Argento's *Trauma* begins with a Rumanian girl, played by the director's young daughter Asia, trying to jump off a bridge in downtown Minneapolis. Unlike Argento's previous heroines, "Aura Petrescu" comes with a lot of emotional baggage—perhaps because it's an "American" film —bourgeois conventions of characterization imposed onto a purer cinema? . . . She's escaped from the Faraday Clinic, she's suffering from bulimia, which the film treats as a visionary gift, like the (false?) mediumship of her mother, the grand European Piper Laurie, doing a great Grace Zabriskie imitation in gypsy shawls and jeweled hairpins.

Bulimia, the rush to evacuate, the ecstasy of revulsion, the insane thrust of the pure—counterpoised to the TV news world of Aura's new American boyfriend—the world which sucks everything in and is hungry for more, more info, more pictures, more drugs and sex. How unflatteringly photographed is Aura's rival, the older, jaded anchorwoman played by Laura Johnson! She's seen in bed in a dark room, yet a harsh strange light reveals tons of acne scars, while her lips move with vulgar inanities. Bulimia here is a mark of European cultivation and old world mystery, yet also as a uniquely American stigmata: as the pompous pal reminds us, "there are four million of these girls *in this country.*"

Naturally the casting of Piper Laurie as the evil mother calls De Palma's film of *Carrie* to mind. Every other scene in *Trauma* seems to be missing, but the music throbs on and on, like a sewing machine drilling a seam, a rhythm, into the scraps of plot. And oh those secondary characters! Okay, they're all victims, but they're kooky, vivid, "multicultural" in fact— escaped from an Altman picture, their lives the fluttery captivity narratives America serves up to the foreign cineaste like doughnuts.

Naturally it wouldn't be an Argento film without one of those "I saw something important I can't remember" elements to dig furrows of worry and loss into its heroine's smooth brow. Bulimia as escape from memory, and food as experience, the greasy diner food shared with the boy in reel one a revolting counterpart to seeing your mother dangle the head of your dad next to her face in reel two, in a dark thicket, with sheets of pink rain pouring down, a wood so dark and cold Oberon and Titania have fled it. The mad doctor who imprisons Aura in his clinic feeds her the magic berry juice from *A Midsummer's Night Dream* and all she can recall is her father leaning down to kiss her. "The bulimic may have recurrent dreams," the narrator tells us. "Her father will be leaning down to kiss her."

Half of event is therapy. The killer lives next door to a little blond boy who plays with insects; a butterfly watches him play and we see the boy from the butterfly's point of view. The boy follows the butterfly through the shuttered window of the killer's house, in broad daylight, and discovers the wooden box in which she stores the Noose-o-Matic. The Noose-o-Matic, slipped around the victim's neck, tightens a razor-sharp string when a button is pushed; kind of a portable guillotine, but very, very Black and Decker, and of course it's never explained how a woman of Piper Laurie's ancestry and dementia has the Rube Goldberg machine shop background to invent such a northern tool. We're not talking efficiency, for the Noose-o-Matic leaves its victim's heads messy on motel room floors, still gasping a last few words when discovered by police (like Z-Man, in Russ Meyer's *Beyond the Valley of the Dolls*). We're talking about how people talk after death, in the realm of Spicer's low ghost. The other half of event is trauma—you could cut my head off, I will still manage a talking cure; birth itself, in a hospital room in a power outage, can be traumatic; how about if your mother shackles you in a basement cage and clearly prefers your dead brother? Watching Argento makes one realize what a child one has always been and is always likely to remain, and how deeply one wants that child dead or snatched. Like the dulled, shocked witnesses of your UFO abduction poem, the child invariably draws the simplest conclusions from the surging tumult of culture. *I was taken by an alien intelligence. My food is trying to poison me. A serial killer is on a "rampage."*

Why take the heads anyway? I guess to give yourself an alibi or to plant them on the dupe mad doctor. Are all those heads going to give me back my Nicholas? I want to avoid having sex with my graphic artist boyfriend. I'll arrange it so my food spews out of me like ectoplasm as I race around the corner to the nearest public toilet—spilling in front of me, projectile as an erection, but fluid, dashed with light and color, like a lava lamp. In despair the child says, I'll do everything I can but it still won't be enough! Love,

                                                        Kevin